Bipolar Balancing Act

Bipolar Balancing Act

Journeying through the valleys and peaks of manic-depression (through the eyes of two who have been there)

Rich and Carol Melcher

Writers Club Press
San Jose New York Lincoln Shanghai

Bipolar Balancing Act
Journeying through the valleys and peaks of manic-
depression (through the eyes of two who have been there)

Writers Club Press
an imprint of iUniverse, Inc.

For information address:
iUniverse, Inc.
5220 S. 16th St., Suite 200
Lincoln, NE 68512
www.iuniverse.com

ISBN: 0-595-22755-4

Printed in the United States of America

Thanks to our parents, families,
friends and doctors who have
guided and encouraged us along
our paths.

~ *Introduction* ~

You need only claim
the events of your life to make
yourself yours.
> *Florida Scott Maxwell*

Imagine taking a pill that caused you to swing emotionally between a depressed and an elated state—back and forth, each day or week or month? Would you ever gamble at taking such a pill to seek enjoying the highs, at the cost of possible depression?

People who have ***bipolar affective disorder*** (also known as *bipolar, or manic-depression...to be used interchangeably)* take prescription drugs to *NOT* experience such swings. Bipolar is a mood disorder (a dysfunction of the neurotransmitters in the human brain) which can cause dramatic mood fluctuations—from deep depression to sky-high mania, and everything in between. Bipolar affects hundreds of thousands (if not millions) of people, not just those who have the illness, but the loved ones and friends who encounter those suffering from the illness.

Bipolar Balancing Act takes you on the journeys of two people brought together by a unique commonality—they both have manic-depression. Two journeys quickly became one, starting the evening they met in June of 1997. Not only is bipolar an open topic with them, it is a unifying force in their relationship.

Each chapter is filled with honest and revealing accounts of their struggles with, and triumphs over bipolar. The chapters begin and end with Rich's poetry (marked by his pen name, "*jacob*"), and offer stories, insights, quotes and practical hints that may be of use to those who have bipolar—or encounter those who do.

Bipolar Balancing Act is a testimony to <u>all</u> people with disabilities (and those who love and care about them) that life can be good—even *VERY* good—for those who have disabilities…if only we reach out and put forth our best effort. We hope this book will be informative and helpful to you.

Bipolar Balancing Act: OUTLINE

Forward

Rich and Carol Melcher have become "stigma busters" in opening their significant life journeys for our enrichment. Through their experiences, they know the paralyzing lows of depression and the erratic highs of mania.

Their autobiographies personalize the struggles of nearly two and one-half million Americans who are diagnosed with Bipolar Affective Disorder. From their writing, persons who share this diagnosis, or mental health professionals, or indeed all of us are challenged by two incredibly courageous and wise authors.

~ They turn mental illness "on its head" as an advantage to deepen one's personhood.

~ They challenge all of us who are married to see our unique problems as opportunities for growth.

~ Their stories demonstrate the wisdom to know and be connected to our 'authentic inner selves' and not be discouraged by external distractions.

~ They articulate sound principles of mental health in clear biographical and poetic sketches.

As readers, we are invited to a feast of personal and marital narratives that are 'parables of faith' which truly inspire. Enjoy!

Dick Fowler, PhD
Licensed Psychologist

Chapter One: Rich's Story

what is it
this energy
this spark of life
which sometimes leaves us
and sometimes overwhelms us
where is the balance between the glory light
and the pit of darkness
this "illness" of manic-depression
is really an oversensitivity
to the glory of life
and the cliff of despair
in-between-ness
is what we seek
to be in control, yet appropriately
vulnerable
to be insightful, but not
in delusion,
to be happy
yet challenging life to
be more

> balance is what we seek
> what we **all** seek
> and walk that tight rope we will
> steadied by the balancing bar
> of good habits, healthy risking
> and gratitude for the
> opportunities
> to live and learn
>
> jacob (Rich)

Have you ever caught yourself in a lie? Or, at least, a self-deception? It can be personally devastating if your foundation of self-esteem is rather shaky, as mine was quite rickety, as a young man at the age of 17, in January 1980. It was the start of a new decade and midpoint of my senior year at Buffalo (Minnesota) High School.

My ego had been padded recently, by being voted captain of the Buffalo High hockey team, best dressed and most likely to succeed—the latter two "honors" conferred by my peers for the yearbook. Just a month earlier, I had been having some difficulty getting to sleep—anxious and unsettled, but it had subsided until late January of 1980—when the dam broke.

I brought my girlfriend home after a Buffalo basketball game and when I got home, something pulled me to sit in the La-z-boy chair. I sat and thought deeply for a few minutes…and, suddenly, like a lightening bolt striking my head, I realized that, although I had told my attractive girlfriend that I *loved her*—I didn't! Immediately I began questioning if I knew how to love at all…my mind began spinning its wheels: "If I don't love her, how can I love my parents? Or my brothers and sisters? Or my friends?…" And within five minutes my mind was spinning down like a fighter plane hit by enemy fire—and I plummeted into the beginnings of depression. I say "beginnings of depression" because, although this was a confusing and painful discovery, it was just a slice of the bitter pie of grief I was to taste.

The half moon crept across the winter sky that night as I didn't sleep a wink, thoughts racing like a stampede of bison. The next morning I went to school with a cavernous feeling beneath my ribs, …the games had begun—the games of how to fake-out people that I was the same happy-go-lucky kid I had been—to fake that I was OK when my heart had been broken and my mind weakened.

> *To live without hope is to*
> *cease to live.*
> *Dostoyevski*

From January to June, 1980, my moods shifted from slouching mediocrity to confused indecision, to tortured suicidal. I was protected from suicidal thoughts and feelings until mid-March because, being the captain of the hockey team, I had responsibility, I was active and I was interacting socially. But when hockey ended in March 1980, I took a nose dive into the dark depths of self-destruction and self-hatred.

I made it through a painful graduation and into the summer where something surprising and marvelous happened…I began working (for the third straight summer) at my father's construction company. At first it may seem like, "yeah, so what?" but it was truly a life-changing experience.

Three important happenings occurred in that summer of 1980 at Dad's company…first, since I no longer had "THE EYES" watching me (the eyes of the students and teachers at my high school), I no longer had to put on my *Rich Melcher happy-go-lucky face*; I could finally just be *myself*. Next, I was in an environment familiar to me—I had worked on the job with those men before. I didn't have to be on guard every moment lest I mess something up—I was careful but not paranoid. And third, unlike most of the time in high school, I could SEE the work of my hands in the tasks I was completing—no matter how menial.

We consider that each problem,
each crisis, is our necessary
preparation for moving another
step down the road.
　　　　　　　unknown

By mid-summer 1980, I was in a strange, in-between place—not quite depressed nor truly feeling myself. In August, upon taking a trip to Montana, Wyoming and Colorado with seven high school friends, my mood swung into ecstacy—the freedom, the natural beauty of the forests and wildlife, the feeling that I wanted to live again...I was alive and free! Meanwhile, although I did not notice or understand it at the time, I was a royal pain in the butt to the other seven travelers; in my manic exuberance; my behaviors were extreme and irritating—no one could tell me anything. I've only come across these truths in personal reflection, over the years—I was oblivious to them at the moment, a common occurrence to one with manic-depression, I believe.

Coming back from the trip, my mother became increasingly concerned about my accelerated behavior and rapid speech patterns. I began writing checks with my new checkbook, buying new clothes, a boom box and even a pair of tennis shoe roller skates. I joined the football squad at Mankato State University (in southern Minnesota) and roller skated nearly everywhere but on the field.

It seemed that all I wanted was attention—the direct opposite of how I had isolated myself during depression. My mother had been with me throughout the depressive times and saw this extremely opposite behaviors as more than peculiar. So she insisted that I go to a mental health clinic in the Twin Cities where I was soon diagnosed as having manic-depression—bipolar affective disorder. I was given lithium and traveled back to Mankato, where I was about to begin my freshman year of college.

> *An easy life teaches nothing.*
> *(fortune cookie)*

My first full-cycle episode took nine months and nearly killed me. My health was at stake for years to come because no one made it clear to me that I had a "serious and persistent mental illness." In fact, I don't remember hearing the term *mental illness* until the personally explosive year of 1986. I thought that the 1980 bout was a one-time occurrence—a single-shot pistol…in no way did I know it was a machine gun with unlimited ammunition, with the safety "off."

In January of 1986, after 5 years of relatively good health, the walls-came-a-tumbling-down, all around me. In short, it was the worst year of my life! Starting with high stress in a no-win situation as a volunteer teacher, in Milwaukee, Wisconsin, I rose quickly into mania.

> *Discomfort is often a bridge,*
> *not a barrier, to success.*
>   ***unknown***

It was a roller coaster year, from mania to depression, to deeper depression, to mania again and even higher (psychotic) mania. Being hospitalized six times in a 12-month period, feeling totally helpless about finding balance…it was the first time in my life that I "thought I was nuts" and that I was condemned to a life of being overtaken by this treacherous illness.

In late 1986, while highly manic, I rushed from my home state of Minnesota to my adopted home state of Wisconsin where I had been a volunteer teacher in Milwaukee from '84-'86, trying to rediscover the success I had experienced earlier with my teaching positions in Milwaukee's Central City. I quickly found that forcing myself on people—no matter how close we once were—was a grave mistake.

Thanks to a priest friend from the parish of my first teaching job in Milwaukee in 1984-85, I made my way safely to a hospital and began my journey down another lonely street on the highway to recovery.

Low-grade depression accompanied me as I found my way back to Minnesota in June of 1987. I worked again at my dad's construction company—this time not just for a summer, but for 2 straight years. This was the longest I had ever worked for *any* company before. Partly because of some personal conflict with my father, and partly because of a destructive mechanism in my psyche and heart (namely, stuffed, unresolved anger), I had my most psychotic mania episode in August of 1989.

Tension between my father and me had been building all summer and late one stormy Friday night in August the flood gates opened and I became destructive.

That day, I had quit my job at my dad's construction company, making a horrendous scene, peeling out of the parking lot in my pick-up. Later, my mom and my dad's business partner met with me and my psychiatrist —I was still in a huff and extremely manic. They decided it would be best for me to stay with my mom that night and then check into a hospital the next day…big mistake! I went home to Buffalo (MN) and was recording tapes for "this book I had been writing"…(a compilation of readings and personal poetry that I thought somehow was going to save the world). But the big dreams turned into a horror story for my mother when at 3 a.m. I began to systematically destroy my fathers' belongings in the street and yard. I had motives, such as smashing the piano bench in the street because my father made me take piano lessons which I hated, when I was in junior high. I was out of control and my mother probably felt endangered and called the police. When the cop came in the house and saw the devastation, he handcuffed me— although I was no longer violent—and brought me to the hospital because I had cut my foot in the rampage. This outburst, this self-expression through destruction earned me a ticket to commitment proceedings and a trip to a state hospital.

"State hospital? That must have been a scary experience!?" Exactly opposite! It was the most productive (and enjoyable) hospitalization I've ever had! The golden maple leaves displayed the splendor of my favorite season at the very time that "the wall" fell in Berlin. For accountability and responsibility's sake, they gave me a job running the huge dishwasher in the kitchen from 7-9 a.m. It was a momentous time also, because I had three major awakenings that fall 1989…I came to realize the importance of physical exercise in keeping my health vibrant while swimming in the pool. This is still a part of my balancing act eleven years later, although getting proper exercise is not always an easy venture.

> *You'd be amazed what you*
> *can take when your purpose*
> *is clear.*
> *(fictional Martin*
> *Luther King in*
> *"The Meeting")*

Next, while talking to a social worker (a "psych tech," to be specific), he stopped me in mid-sentence: "Wait, Rich,…you are a person first! You are a *person* with a mental illness, NOT a mentally ill person!"

No one had ever given me that level of dignity before, nor the insight that I was more powerful and important than this illness. That conversation gave me a new confidence and an enriched outlook.

The third awakening I had at the state hospital evolved when someone suggested that I begin to write down my specific symptoms that become obvious when I begin to get manic. So I started writing, and reflecting, and writing some more. Eventually, I came up with 52 "manic clues" (as I have come to call them). Here is a taste:

Manic Clues

1. *URGENCY*
2. *heightened energy*
3. *tunnel vision*
4. *DESTRUCTIVE TO RELATIONSHIPS*
5. *driving faster/recklessly*
6. *very manipulative*
7. *disturbed ability to make rational decisions*
8. *destructive of things*
9. *"don't get in my way!"*
10. *sleeping/eating changes*

(For the complete list, turn to the appendix). Being aware of these clues has given me at least **some** power in dealing with bipolar. There have also been times—since the fall the of '89—when I was not aware of my manic clues at all...and the result was disastrous! (Chapter five will give you an extended look at how dangerous it can be for me to be unaware of my manic clues).

Each chapter of <u>Bipolar Balancing Act</u>, as mentioned in the introduction, will contain at least one acronym—a memory-friendly way of giving pithy ideas that pertain to the topic at hand.

WAGS is the acronym for chapter one, and it stands for...

<u>W</u>e've
<u>A</u>ll
<u>G</u>ot
<u>S</u>omething

...something such as an illness, a disability, a stutter, a scar, a dysfunctional past...everyone has *something*—and this can be <u>good,</u> in that, it *levels the playing field*. You see, if everyone has **some** defect, we can find unity in our "brokenness."

A few years ago, while attending a 12-Step (Al-Anon) group, I was talking to the group about how wonderful it is that we are all so *unique*, differently made, with varied gifts. I spoke for about 5-10 minutes about this before a group member raised her hand and said, "Being unique is OK, but being 'terminally unique' can cause much pain." She gave me the tools to create the most profound idea I have ever put to paper... "I believe we are **unique in our gifts and united in our struggles.**"

I have come to believe this with all my heart. Just in the realm of manic-depression, it seems that no matter who my wife Carol and I talk to, they are either dealing with this illness or know someone who is. Yet I do not see my illness as a deficit...I see it as an opportunity to learn and grow—to discover the *true meaning of life*.

Stephen Covey, author of <u>The Seven Habits of Highly Effective People</u>, challenges readers to write their epitaph—what they would want to appear on their gravestone...mine is quite simple and is my current *true meaning of life*... "Rich learned from and grew with *whatever* he was given and joyfully gave it back."

This encompasses my feelings and thoughts about the importance of *knowing yourself,* knowing your weak areas, your struggles, your preferences and your strengths. Having manic-depression has forced me to think and feel deeper than I would have had to if I never had the illness. Illness CAN BE a blessing.

everything is poem
when mania creeps out
of its damp, dark, mold-filled cave
so delighted to see its own reflection
in pen & purpose
purple passion
leaks out of old wineskins of depression and
captivity

yet poem is not as important as poet
the words in volley are mere expression of self
not self
itself

manic trains of thought with no apparent track
wind among the smoky hills of a deeper mind
sometimes leaving engineer behind in dust
and gravel

hope lies in bending of rails to bring the iron horse
back home again
to rest in the station of peace
awaiting freight of less weight
and passengers of promise

jacob

Chapter Two: Carol's Story

individuality
is not a choice
it's a fact
in order to truly be
A PART OF
you need to be
apart from

the imitator always ends up less
because the true self is hidden
and only in living in the self
can one truly be **free**

self-knowledge & self-discovery appear to be the only ways
to find the true self
for integrity & wisdom — inner strengths —
will shine brightly in the person
who has found the self
the inner navigator

loneliness is actually
the inability to be satisfied with self
and to NEED others in order to be whole –
true relationship only happens between
those who have planted seeds in
discovery-soil (and have made peace with themselves)
acquiring the space and time to **become**
…becoming themselves in the solitude of heart and mind
a distance that allows one to see inside
for truth and purpose –
only then approaching outer-life once more
renewed   awakened   alive

jacob

I was the youngest of three sisters and then, when I was five, my mother brought home our baby brother, the son my parents had long awaited. Memories of growing up on the outskirts of Delano, a small central Minnesota town, are fond. Childhood recollections are filled with countless adventures spawned by my two best friends' and my creative imagination and endless thirst for adventure. An old school bus, converted into a camper by my father, became the family adventure mobile known as the "Flying Dutchman". Off we went every summer on countless journeys that took us from one coast to the other, exploring far away, unknown destinations. To this day, I count these times among my most treasured memories and am always up for a road trip to places yet unexplored.

The years of my schooling gave me the chance to participate in speech, chorus, band, drama, sports, cheerleading and a host of other school-sponsored activities. I was always looking to be involved in any and all scholastic and extra-curricular activities...to be a part of, to be the best...to belong.

Very early in life, I discovered that I loved to sing. My first solo performance was in the

Christmas program in the first grade. This "stellar" debut proved to be the first of many solo spots in weddings, funerals, musicals, choirs and other "gigs." To this day, music continues to play a big part in my life.

The fall after graduating from high school, I headed off to college as a music major and art minor, in a small private college in central Minnesota. I found myself among a large number of talented students who proved to be stiff competition for parts in ensembles and roles in musicals. I no longer felt like the "creme de la crop," as I had in my small, home town productions. This was the first of many humbling experiences during my first year of college.

The summer following my freshman year, Dorita, my best college buddy and I got summer jobs together in Alexandria, a mid-western Minnesota resort town. When it came time to return to school, the fall of 1974, we decided we weren't ready to go back to school. We felt a yearning to experience the "real world." Three weeks into our sophomore year, we quit school and set out to find jobs in Minneapolis.

The true self is always in motion,
like music, a river of life,
changing, moving, failing
suffering, learning, shining.
Brenda Ueland

Needless to say, our parents were less than thrilled with our decision to do the "Laverne and Shirley" thing and leave our college plans behind. But we were certain, being "mature nineteen year old adults," that we knew what was best for our lives and that we were going to get out on our own and experience the *real* world as working women.

Our job search landed jobs at the same company, which was important as we only had one car between us—Dorita's '63 Ford station wagon. We found an efficiency apartment, modestly priced (still slightly beyond our means) and set up our lives in the "real world" with a menagerie of borrowed furniture and household items. I will never forget the two roll away beds we kept in the closet and drug out in which to sleep every night in our little apartment.

By the spring of 1975, Dorita decided she had had enough of the working world and was ready

to give school another try. She was going to regis-
ter for fall quarter and return to the central
Minnesota college. Not feeling that I was ready to
go back to school yet, I decided to stay in the
cities, by myself, and continue to work.

That fall, Dorita returned to college. For the
first time in my life, I was on my own—alone—
and not feeling very good about it. A very strong
friendship bond and dependence on Dorita's
companionship had developed throughout the
past two years. Her leaving created a huge hole in
my life. For the first time, I was truly alone and on
my own in the big, bad, cruel, scary world. Now
that I was without my best friend, feelings of
being trapped, lonely and isolated could not be
shaken.

> *Real difficulties can be*
> *overcome...it is only the*
> *imaginary ones that are*
> *unconquerable*
> *Theodore N. Vail*

If only I had a car, I thought, I wouldn't feel so
confined. I was getting a ride to work from
another individual at the apartment complex that
worked with me. This was about the only opportunity I had to get out of the apartment, other

than the landlord letting me ride to the grocery store with her to get my weekly provisions.

I had to get over these feelings that were eating away at me. If only I could get home to my parents' house on the weekends, about a half hour away, I would not feel so..."depressed."

As it turned out, every weekend, my father would swing by the apartment and bring me home for the weekend. It felt very good to be home. I felt very secure and safe...but I still felt this lonely pit in my gut. Perhaps, the pit of regret for not returning to school with Dorita. Maybe I was missing all those newly-found friendships at college, and wishing I were a part of all the activities of which I was missing out. Being in the working world, on my own at age 20, was not an adventure anymore, it had become a nightmare.

> *We must accept finite*
> *disappointments, but we must*
> *never lose infinite hope.*
> *Martin Luther King, Jr.*

Each time my father would drop me off at the apartment, it became more and more difficult to say good bye and watch him drive away. I was so lonely, but I thought, "I chose this path so I need to stick it out until I have another game plan." Thoughts about going back to school were constantly in the back of my mind, but my lack of confidence kept me from moving forward with my life and getting a new action plan in motion.

In January of 1976, I moved out of my apartment and home to live with my parents. It felt so good to be home, but still those feelings of loneliness, helplessness and insecurity still haunted me.

Soon after my move home, I was in the firm, ugly grip of depression. Work became unbearable. Even the simple, routine, daily tasks of my job became difficult and stress-ridden. I could barely get myself out of bed in the morning, because I dreaded facing another day of work. My co-workers had seen me change from a pleasingly plump, bubbly outgoing energetic young lady to a gaunt, repressed, quiet, insecure, anxiety-ridden person. Finally, I told my parents I could not go back to work.

They tried every thing to get me out of this funk. They included me in on all of their outings, and suggested I get together with some of my friends that were still in town. They also encouraged me to go across the street to see my childhood buddies, even called some of my friends who I'd been avoiding, to have them invite me along to the beach...anything to get me to reach out, to get out of the house...to become the "old bubbly Carol" I used to be. But something strange inside of me, held me back, kept me at bay, covered my emotions in a smoky black veil and kept me hiding out in my parents house..."*safe...safe*, yes," I thought. I will be OK and *safe*, if I can just stay here at "home," the only secure place I knew in my life, at the time.

cocoon
wrap me up in silk
spin me a home
to comfort
me
I
want
a warm
dark, quiet
place that exists
only to serve my needs
a place where I feel safe
a place where I can grow and
change in my own space, silent
comfortable

jacob

A noticeable weight loss pattern (always struggling with weight *gain*) was noticed by my parents and other acquaintances. I was now 114 pounds and 5' 8" tall...another red flag which worried my parents.

Not knowing where else to turn, they made an appointment for me with a psychologist. "What good could she do for me?," I thought. Though numerous visits throughout the early spring and summer revealed no specific diagnosis, anti-depressants were promptly prescribed.

Dad and Mom could see that it was anti-pro-ductive for me to be sitting (and mostly sleeping) around the house all day and thought if I got a job, I would start feeling better about myself. Doing *something* would certainly be better than my current hermit-like existence I was displaying in their home.

Fine. So *what* and *where* does an extremely depressed young person find work? A toy factory was hiring summer workers. My friend Mary Jo was working there and Mom called and arranged for me to catch a ride to work.... *if* I got the job.

Assembly line work...no skills required, other than having a pulse...I got the job.

The summer months, on the assembly line, were a blur. I worked the second shift—3 p.m. to midnight. I'd get home from work about 1 a.m., go to bed, sleep until noon or later, get up, shower, eat a little lunch, and wait to be picked up for another night at the factory. I remember the isolation I felt, not knowing any of the people I worked with and not having enough confidence to reach out to get to know them. This was clearly atypical for me. Lunch breaks were spent by myself, hoping no one would talk to me so I could stay isolated, trapped in my own tormented thoughts, and dwell on my loneliness and despair.

As the summer pressed on, I had to make some decisions about my life. *If* I wanted to go on *living*, do I continue to work at this hell hole, or do I force myself to go back to school and try to function in the environment I once thrived in, when I was "my old self"? I just wanted to be able to be *somewhere* that I could feel "normal" again and was hoping a change of environment would resurrect the *me* I used to know and felt good about.

> *I guess it comes to a simple*
> *choice…get busy livin'*
> *or get busy dyin'!*
> *Andy Dufresne*
> *(The Shawshank Redemption)*

The decision was made. In September of 1976, I returned to my college. The first three weeks were very scary. I was greeted by many familiar faces, but had difficulty getting reacquainted because I did not *feel* like the same person they knew my freshman year. I was the antithesis of my usual, bubbly self…shy, introverted, withdrawn, quiet…the one thing most people noticed was my drastic weight loss. I had been a size 13 freshman year, and now I was about a size 3.

Needless to say, the guys noticed the "new," slender me immediately. I had invitations for dates left and right. At first, I turned them down, not feeling up to dating, but soon my feeling started to shift. I started feeling pretty good about the attention I was being shown.

By early October, three weeks into the school year, I had come out of my "funk" and was partying, dating and having the time of my life. My hunger had returned and I was putting on weight (a little too quickly). My artistic juices for painting and drawing had been reawakened and flowed freely. I spent hours painting enlarged posters of popular album covers for friends to hang on their dorm room walls. I was a *busy* girl...busy feeling great (something I had not felt for months) and living life to an extreme. Busy—I *much* too busy *living*, celebrating my "reawakening"—to go to my classes.

I purchased a huge stereo system, an abundance of albums, a whole new wardrobe for the new, slender me, including all the accessories. Needless to say, my checking account had become severely overextended

How could my roommate *dare* say I was acting strange (I had just returned from hitchhiking to Moorhead, about 175 miles away, and back, to visit a friend and go to a rock concert). She had called my parents and told them I had not been attending classes, had not been sleeping much, and that she feared I was heading on a collision course to a breakdown of some kind.

Breakdown? Wait a minute! I thought I had just gotten fixed! I felt *great*. I felt that I was living life to its fullest and *nothing* was going to stop me from having these great experiences and feelings. I had just been through six months of depression (prison) and now I was finally...FREE!!

My parents called and said the dean of my school had called them. He was concerned that I had not been attending classes and indicated that, in order to avoid failing grades for the semester, I would need to withdraw from school.

A sliver of reality hit me and I realized the party was over. My parents came up to school and helped me pack up my belongings. I couldn't understand why they were so upset. Here I was feeling so good, and I thought that was what they had wanted for me all those months that I had struggled with depression.

My parents called the psychologist that I had been seeing in Minneapolis and described the drastic "mood swing" I had experienced. She immediately referred me to a respected psychiatrist who recommended I be admitted to the hospital for evaluation and treatment.

We consider that each problem,
each crisis, is our necessary
preparation for moving another
step down the road.
Unknown

I spent the next two weeks in the hospital. I was diagnosed and treated for manic-depressive illness (bipolar disorder) and slowly came down from the rafters.

My first feeling about the illness, was, "*WHY ME???*" I hated taking medication. It made me thirsty and groggy, and I didn't want to accept the fact that I would have to take this medication, possibly, for the rest of my life!!

How would I explain this to my friends, the ones I left behind at college and my home town buddies. How could I ever explain my behavior and try to repair some of the friendships that may have been destroyed by my erratic behavior. What man will ever accept me (and my illness) and want to be my life partner? Where does my life go from here? How do I start over *again?*

*I could choose to see this situation as a setback
or a starting point.*
W. *Mitchell*

The acronym for Chapter 2 is **MOTOR**:

Moving (from)
Obstacles
To
Opportunities,
Relentlessly

Over the past 20 plus years, I have learned
many valuable lessons in coping with the obstacles and challenges of mental illness. The most
substantial opportunities for growth in knowledge and self-determination have taken place
after traveling through the valleys and peaks of
bipolar illness.

For the next several years, I floated in and out
of a number of jobs and career possibilities, but
nothing seemed to fit right. I had lived in a few
apartments with friends but ended up back at my
parents house for lack of adequate funds.

In November of 1980, a close friend who had
been living and working out in Montana, at Big

Sky Ski Resort, called and encouraged me to "test my wings" and come out to Montana. She had connections to getting me a job at Big Sky Resort, and I jumped at the opportunity to "get out of Dodge" and make it on my own, without burdening my parents any longer.

December 21st, 1980, I headed west, driving my friend's compact car out to Montana, which she had left at her parents' in our home town. I arrived on Christmas Eve and started working as a dishwasher in the lodge, the very next day.

Life on the mountain was simple, wages were very modest, but it felt good to be on my own. By the next spring, I was ready to search for a "real" job and moved to Bozeman, about 40 miles away. I spent the next three years working various jobs to keep my head above water. During those three years I stayed pretty healthy, emotionally, except for one bout with depression. I had not been taking my medications faithfully and found myself severely depressed and on the verge of needing to be hospitalized. With the support of some very good friends and my psychiatrist, I made it out of the woods and back on track again.

The ongoing goal for me has been to create something positive from the struggles I have had with mental illness. I have had the opportunity to share my illness with individuals going through similar situations which has helped them understand and better cope with their circumstances. This is one of the ways I have used **MOTOR** in my life—assisting others in their time of need.

In the sixth chapter, I will share the most life-changing lesson that I had to learn, and am still learning...*balance*.

> *the journey has been long*
> *and the path winding*
> *when the brilliant orange sun goes down*
> *this feeling of incompleteness*
> *veils the splendid scene*
> *and the search*
> *(search for contentment and purpose)*
> *goes on*
> *stumbling upon the rocks*
> *of despair and frustration*
> *tears hide in the channels*
> *of a deeper mind*
> *where all is symbol and emotion ~*
> *there is peace*
> *no matter the chaos of daily life*

there is a serene meandering stream
which flows deep within
quenching the thirst of a longing
unexplained
to live more fully
to be authentic
to be fully alive

jacob

Chapter Three: The Meeting

in this life of mine
there is one thing I most want
a loved one to be there, and here
as the drama unfolds
this would be my greatest loss in life
if I were not to have become the me
I'm supposed to be
because there was no interaction,
no one to hear me in times of confusion and pain
in times of glee and fulfillment
to help me see it, feel it and pull it all together
"I" would not be, without this gentle,
firm confrontation and interaction
what a loss it would be not have to become me
sometimes I think the only way this could happen
this creation of self
would be with a significant other
a wife, to be committed to, to be loyal to
but sometimes I wonder if this is my calling
seeing that it hasn't happened yet

but I struggle on with the questions
and thank God for what I've been given

jacob

Surprisingly, the auditorium was 2/3 full, possibly 150-200 people looking on for the evening's events—one activity being my talk. I was to speak on "Knowing yourself, through the good times, the bad times and the ho-hum times..." I had never spoken at a Christian singles group gathering before and really didn't know what to expect.

> *If we were able to see the*
> *big picture, we'd greet all*
> *situations, large and small,*
> *with a thankful heart.*
> ***Each Day A New Beginning***

The talk, which was supposed to last 40 minutes (or, at least, that's how long the meeting planner had expected me to talk) only lasted 20 minutes...OOPS! I guess a guy like me can make a mistake on speech length once in a while. I remember only mentioning that I had manic-depression and reflecting on it for about two minutes during the talk. The evening soon took on an unexpected tone.

As my speech ended and I asked if anyone had a question or comment, I remember a long 10 seconds of silence. It was getting a bit unnerving, when, suddenly, a red-headed gal in the front row, off to my left, spoke up… "It looks like we have a big crowd tonight,…" as she scanned the group to her left, "but that's OK. I have manic-depression too and…" For the next minute or two, we bantered back and forth—a mini-conversation about mutual experiences with the illness —until she said, "Well, maybe we should continue this over coffee some other time." Spontaneously I shot back, "Oh, is this our *FIRST date*?" The crowd roared, knowing her to be the spunky, outgoing leader of the worship band that played at these functions.

> *When we look for the good*
> *in others we discover the best*
> *in ourselves.*
> *Martin Walsh*

Then, for the next 45 minutes (or more), the crowd was awakened to an opportunity that doesn't occur everyday—a chance to talk openly and honestly about a stigmatized aspect of our culture—mental illness. The participants asked me questions about bipolar, making comments about family members and friends who have the illness. I see now that the avalanche of interaction that night happened only because the red-head had the courage to share about her illness so openly.

After the event, the red-head found me in the crowd and introduced herself as "Carol". I was delighted to meet such a vivacious, attractive woman, yet we didn't get to speak much because other participants were buzzing around me with more questions and comments about the topic. So I decided that I would see Carol again, this time as a participant in the next singles gathering the following month.

Three weeks later, there was Carol leading the worship band, guitar in hand, joyful and bubbly as ever. But before I could ask her out, she came up to me and said, "So, when are we going to have that coffee?" And the romance was launched. We began dating the next week and we soon became soul partners. Because we were "older" (I was 36 and Carol 42) and knew what we were looking for in a mate, we became "serious" very soon and were engaged in three months. Carol and I were married in March of 1998 and headed to Costa Rica for our honeymoon.

One of the bridges that many people with a psychological/emotional disability must cross when dating is: *When do I tell him or her that I have "xyz" disability?* With us, that bridge had been crossed in our first encounter and never became an issue.

> *Mystery means you don't*
> *know all the answers, but*
> *you're continuing the journey*
> *anyhow.*
>   *jacob*

Carol and I were able to talk about manic-depression openly—in fact, it became one of our frequent topics of conversation. I had been doing public speaking about the illness for 5 years, so it was natural for me to talk about it—and Carol chimed right in. Also, since 1990 I had been working for a mental health firm that primarily employed and housed people with mental illness, so I had day to day contact with the mental health field. This organization, *Tasks Unlimited*, based in Minneapolis, took me on as a janitor in 1990 and groomed me into a manager from 1995-1998. *Tasks* provided an opportunity to be on the governing board and offered many recreational activities. I learned numerous management skills and, at one point, supervised a crew of 20 janitors at an area federal building. It was the perfect situation at the perfect time in my life...when I needed responsibility and challenge, they provided the structure and the circumstances. My hat's off to "*Tasks!*"

It is a funny thing about life—
if you refuse to accept anything
but the best, you often get it.
Somerset Maugham

Besides *Tasks*, one of the greatest advantages in my life during the '90s (something I didn't have in the early-to-mid '80s) was the awareness that I had a "serious and persistent mental illness." This may sound strange—why would someone WANT to know this? Well, if a tiger is on my tail, I'd rather know it so I can deal with it, rather that it grabbing a hold of the seat of my pants without warning.

Camaraderie is the theme of this chapter—mainly, the camaraderie that Carol and I have found—being bonded by the illness of manic-depression. The acronym used to describe camaraderie is WAITT:

We're
All
In
This
Together

The unity that two can share brings, as Stephen Covey's "6th Habit" states: SYNERGY. The focus here is on solving problems and sharing the inner-self with the other—which is one of Carol and my greatest strengths.

Still, the most unifying quality of our relationship, besides our spirituality, would certainly be our openness about bipolar...although our ability to use straight talk (open, honest, nonjudgmental sharing) about numerous topics is increasing. Developing this trust comes slower than sharing about bipolar did.

> *The change of one simple behavior can affect other behaviors and change many things.*
> *Jean Baer*

Carol and I ventured out into the deeper waters of better communication by taking a course on couples' communication in fall of '99. It was held on 5 consecutive Monday nights, for 2 hours each evening and gave us ideas and techniques on how to communicate our thoughts, feelings and wants more accurately. Also, we looked at how nonverbal communication can powerfully affect the process of giving and receiving messages. Carol will expand on this more in *chapter six.*

WAITT (*We're All In This Together*)is a part of my philosophy of life (as are all 7 acronyms presented in this book) because it is a mindset of openness and companionship. If you treat people right, and aren't afraid to start conversations with people, you'll never be isolated or bored—even to be bold and confident enough to strike up a conversation while standing in line at the grocery store.

WAITT can open up a lot of doors. There's the story of a woman going for a business interview who, in the lobby of the building in which she was interviewing, gave a friendly smile—for no reason at all—to a gentleman who crossed her path in the lobby. When she got to the interview, she was surprised to find that the man she had smiled at was the interviewer. Never doubt it— the interview went very well.

WAITT-ing on one another can be very beneficial, as Carol and I have found out in our relationship. We're in the same boat, traveling the same sea.

we lock eyes
I share with you
the ME
I'm unable
to see
or maybe
the ME
I have trouble
showing myself
or even
the ME
full of passion &
playfulness
or maybe even
the ME
searching for
significance
acceptance
connectedness ~
but then
you free
inside
the joy
and wonder
as you
give my selves
back to me

touched
loved
heard

jacob

Chapter Four: A Time of Depression

and so
   once again
the hurricane hit the beach
   (never thought I'd see another)
   after all those I've lived through
  the forecast had shown only partly sunny
and yet the gale-force winds of my mind began to swirl
waves of my heart came crashing in
     on the beach, my soul, my personhood
        lost
   once again
   but with a better shelter
  than past storms
     do I fight against the storm
      or ride it out?
    knowing that storms "don't last always"
   (kind of a combination this time)
  trying to straighten out
my trade wind thoughts
   while feeling the heat of depression

don't run away
  face the demons
    but do I face them by trying to change
    or understand
        or just let it be?
            (I really don't know)

jacob

Depression is the ugliest, most painful state that Carol and I have been in. It is like stumbling through a dark, dank tunnel with only a single candle flickering to light the way.

> *You can sit and agonize*
> *until your agony is*
> *your heaviest load.*
> **The Indigo Girls**

In 1986, I suffered from such debilitating depression that I had to have ECT (electro convulsive therapy—"shock therapy") to help pull me out of the steep downward spiral my mind was caught in. I had no hope, no vision of my own goodness, no insight into how this episode could be used to my benefit if I weathered the storm. I had BECOME the storm, instead of a wind-swept boat in the midst of it.

Depression leaves me with no clear or bright (or any) future, and only ashes to trudge through because I'm caught in the negativity and regret over a "faulty" past. The present moments slip away too, because my mind and body can't see or feel the beauty of everyday life.

words to describe my un-in-it-ness

I DON'T CARE
> *screams in my head*
> *high above the city*

> > > *screaming*
> *nobody hears*
> *nobody is meant to hear*

> > *cry hollow, but full*
> *into the nothingness*

> > > *no answer*

> > > > *jacob*

Retrospectively, I wish I could have seen the great goldmine that the depressive states were to become…this goldmine of depression lies in the memory of pain and disillusionment as compared to the somewhat trying moments of everyday life when I'm healthy. Usually it's no contest and the current moments of boredom or anxiety can be put into perspective, and the present can become bearable, if not enjoyable once again. A good part of my joy occurs by contrast to the sorrow and pain I have gone through during my depressive stages.

I've been deeply depressed only twice in my life and both times wound up feeling helpless and hopeless—once in the spring of 1980 and the other time in the spring/summer of 1986. I think my illness kicked-in in 1980 not merely because I had repressed my feelings, but because the illness had ripened on the tree of my physiological evolution. The fruit of manic-depression fell from the tree at the first vigorous shaking. In other words, it was nature <u>and</u> nurture that inevitably concocted my first fall into the pit of despair.

> *Our greatest glory consists*
> *not in never falling, but in*
> *rising every time we fall.*
> *Ralph Waldo Emerson*

In the movie THE WIZ, the African-American version of the Wizard of Oz, the Good Witch of the South, Glinda, *created* the blizzard that swept Dorothy away and into the land of Oz. This is an example of how, as the Chinese put it, *CRISIS* equals *opportunity* as well as danger. During my depressions, my opportunity was to begin to notice the little pleasures and beauty that everyday life has to offer. I believe God guided me in and through the tough times so I could become a more sensitive, compassionate man.

This brings us to the acronym for Chapter 4... *COLA*:

Choosing
   Optimistic
    Loving
     Attitudes

Life is all about attitudes, perspective. One could say that the antithesis of depression is *choice*...the ability to "choose" our emotions by the thoughts we allow to harbor in the bays of our minds. This is the essence of Rational Emotive Therapy (RET)—the belief that what we think creates what we feel.

> *They say*
> *"it's all in your attitude"*
> *and it's true*
> *you **are** your attitudes*
> *your thoughts are your landscape*
> *and outlook the color of glass in your lenses*
> *distortions are seen as smudges*
> *capturing too much light*
> *or not letting enough in*

making the glass an opaque a brilliance
if you want to "know thyself"
just run a print-out of your attitudes
*and your **self** will be hard-copy evidence*

jacob

A *COLA moment* occurs in the motion picture "Renaissance Man" as Danny Devito plays a teacher trying to instill knowledge, self-respect and discipline into a group of boot camp washouts in a last-chance class for the U. S. Army. At one point—a teachable moment—Devito affirms an Army motto by pointing to his head and stating, "Victory starts here!"

Indeed, victory starts in the mind of all of us, but so does failure, pride, hatred, fear and ignorance. We have choices in what we think, which creates how we feel. Our minds are the computers—like in the space shuttle Endeavor—you can have a million pounds of thrust (motivation) and a payload of gadgets inside (people skills), but if your computer is malfunctioning (brain), there is little chance that you're going to have a successful mission.

This is why I believe having a mental illness can be so alarming…if the computer has a problem, the entire person is in danger. Whereas, with many conditions (heart trouble, asthma, broken bones) the injury is localized. A mental illness presents an all-encompassing dysfunction, much like the space shuttle with malfunctioning computers. When the brain's affected, EVERY-THING is affected.

> *Everything can be taken from a man but one thing: the last of human freedoms—to choose one's own attitude in any set of circumstances, to choose one's own way.*
> *Viktor Frankl*

I actually came across Rational Emotive Therapy during my agitated, moderately depressed state in summer '86, in a book that I discovered called <u>Feeling Good</u>, by Dr. David Burns. It was the knowledge that I had *choices* and was not a slave of my erratic emotions that was refreshing and led to one of the most crucial turning points in my recovery. Although it didn't cure the depression I had been experiencing, it did give me much-needed *hope*—hope for a life of emotional and psychological security. Eventually the depression lifted and the hope remained within.

Another *COLA* break through occurred in the mid-'90s when I came to understand that, as motivational speaker W. Mitchell put it, *"It's not what happens to you—it's what you do about it!"* It's not the cards you are dealt that matter, but how you play your hand. Carol and I have been dealt a bipolar hand and our choice has been to become "stigma busters" and talk about our mutual illness openly and honestly, rather than hide our truth. As Martin Luther King, Jr., put it, "Unearned suffering is redemptive..." and Carol and I have chosen to declassify our experiences and share how the roller coaster of bipolar has affected us.

Our ability to deal with the illness evolved from thousands of hours of long-suffering with the lethargy of depression and the boiling point of mania. We are better people now because the illness has forced us to make tough choices—be happy rather than sad, embrace rather than suffer, choose gratitude rather than resentment...We thank God we have had manic-depression in our lives *to forge us into who we have become today*. This may sound silly to those of you who have never suffered traumatic events, but good CAN come from the bad events if one chooses to search for the good—to choose *optimism*.

Depression isn't the end of life and COLA isn't a cure-all. But when someone who is depressed finds their way back to balance (through chemical and/or talk therapy) it gives them the opportunity to seek the optimistic viewpoint in every decision they make.

best cure for depression
I've ever found
keep looking for life
around you
noticing every detail

from this
life will spring
if you can express
what you have seen, felt, heard, smelled, tasted

the freedom comes in the
expression of such life
and in allowing
wonder to become
a part of life
once more –
seek life

                          jacob

Chapter Five: A Time of Mania

mania
the drive to
excellence?
sometimes so
but so often the drive down the wrong
side of the street
yet I have salvaged many aspects of my manic creativity
because they are the inner me, the me so deep and personal
that I keep much of it safely tucked away
and still, often. I am tempted to show it to my friends
and family
and I'm learning how to cherish some of the insane realisms
which came out in mad delight and fervor for the moment
the joy of being alive and yet having no clear boundaries
just possibilities, and too little time to create
this is mania—the unbridled glee and artistic qualities
unleashed into the world

*I cannot live this way, but I can hang onto the positive
aspects
as I make them a part of my life
and I go on with life
and life is good*

jacob

In Greek mythology, there is a story of a father, Daedalus, who constructed wings of wax and feathers for himself and his son, Icarus, to escape from the Greek island of Crete. On their flight, Icarus—in his youthful exuberance—soared too high and the dazzling rays of the sun melted the wax on his wings...the wings came apart and he plummeted into the sea to his death.

Such is the nature of mania, not necessarily to "plummet to one's death," but that the highs CAN end up in depression. In fall of 1999, I nearly came to the same end, but Carol was instrumental in assisting me to a safe landing. I have had five major manic phases in my life (whereas I have only had two deep depressive bouts), the most recent manic phase occurring in October 1999. This was a very dangerous, self-hiding episode because I was so socially compe-tent—so believable (at least, to myself).

As youngest of nine (and because of my per-sonality type) I often just followed in my broth-ers' and sisters' footsteps, including how I dealt with anger. Our family rarely expressed anger openly and I often submerged into passive-aggressive anger. I have been dealing with my passive-aggressive ways for years, in counseling and in my relationships. Rather than being above board, passive-aggressive anger shoots torpedoes at the hull of others—unseen, but deadly (sarcasm, getting others back—behind their back, or just stuffing anger into a black hole of unawareness—my most common type).

Therefore, annoyances, dissatisfactions and unstated preferences can become petrified into resentment and build up like in a pressure cooker...many small incidents pressed together becoming explosive. This is what happened in my two-year relationship with Carol...stuffing, jamming it in, suppressing my wants,...

In this state, the hidden anger can, under the surface, have dramatic influence. This phenomenon is the *opposite* of acronym number five—*CAIS:*

> Connectedness (with the)
> Authentic
> Inner
> Self

Connectedness is a life line between my body, mind and spirit, a crucial component of my healthy self. But in September of 1999, my psychiatrist—who I had been seeing for 13 years—retired, and I was forced to seek out another doctor. At my first appointment with my new psychiatrist, I asked if there was another anti-psychotic medication I could take that wouldn't cause weight gain like my current medication did.

Without any of my medical records and not knowing me from Adam, he pulled out a few months worth of samples of a new med that he thought would do the trick. But he simply *told me* the dosage, never writing it down.

Within a week, I wasn't sleeping much, I was highly energetic, showing many of the manic clues—*I was manic*-a place I'd never imagined I'd ever be again…but I was unaware of the precarious condition I was in.

> *I don't have a solution but I*
> *admire your problem.*
> *Glen McDaniel*

When I marched back to my new doctor to get assistance, I discovered that I was only taking 1/3 the correct amount. I immediately got on the correct dosage but that was not enough.

They say that a gasoline tanker truck less than half full, when taking a sharp corner, can set the liquid contents in motion...so that, down the road, even when the truck has straightened out, the sloshing liquid can tip the entire truck over...this is what happened to me. Once my system lost its balance with the med mix up, I lost my connectedness with my authentic inner self (CAIS) and was left hanging from the high wire by my hands.

One of the components of mania can be over-sensitivity. On Friday, October 8, 1999, I became very disturbed by some statements I heard at our Bible study that night. Then, when I confronted Carol about the upsetting words on the way home, she seemed to back up those who I thought were so out of line. In my mind and heart, a sacred trust had been crushed.

I went to bed angry and awoke at 4:30 a.m. with a fearful, agitated, restless feeling and quickly knew I had to get out of the house (it was a feeling that evil was present—a feeling I seem to have only when I am manic). I had to get out of the house and write! So I left Carol a note, saying I needed some *time and space*, and took off to find a "safe" place to write.

I ended up in my hometown, Buffalo, Minn., an hour away, in a restaurant with a notebook and a pen. For the next three hours, I spilled my mind, heart and soul onto 24 pages of paper. The resentments poured out in a grand cathartic release, and yet, even though the stuffed emotions were not all about Carol, she became the focal point of my anger and disappointment.

> *Let your soul guide you along the way.*
> **Sting**

After I finished the 24-pages, I felt I had only 2 choices—"present or resent" (Fight or flee)—present Carol with my findings or not communicate at all and run…my illness chose the latter(and I went along for the ride). The illness can have its way once it gets control. The mania masquerades as a friend, and my friend had just allowed me to spill out my inner self—this must be good, I thought. Actually, "it's what you do with it" that matters, and my mind used the word freedom in place of a more accurate term—*abandonment*. I thought I was being true to myself, utilizing the CAIS acronym, but I had twisted the meaning of truth to fit a manic definition—do whatever you can to get whatever you want. I was now in the grips of the illness, though I didn't realize it yet. My true personality had been covered with a wet blanket and my *manic-personality* was waving high on the flagpole. I was actually a different person with a different operating system—like putting new software in the computer of my mind.

> ***Being genuine is far more***
> ***important than being great.***
> ***Touchstones***

My mind, focusing on some past successes when I had been a volunteer teacher in the Mid-1980s in Milwaukee, took over and I fled to Wisconsin. There I visited my priest friend again who I knew when I was volunteer teacher. He thought it was highly irregular for me to just appear at his doorstep at 10 pm, and insisted I seek medical attention. As it worked out, he helped me get admitted to the same hospital in northern Milwaukee that I had been admitted to when I was first hospitalized in 1986.

At the hospital, I was full of blame and criticism of Carol and even called my parents to make sure CAROL got help. Wow! How blind one can be in this stage of mania. The delusion of health and liberation had a strangle-hold on me. After only two days in the hospital—my ill mind still racing—I left the hospital and was like a whirling dervish of spontaneity. I ended up driving to Des Moines, leaving the car there and catching a flight to Salt Lake City, via Denver. I ended up running out of money and wandering downtown from hotel to hotel. Luckily, I contacted Carol and she arranged for me to catch a flight home in the morning—with assistance from the hotel management and the gate workers at the Salt Lake City airport. Dazed and confused, I made it to Minneapolis where one of my brothers and Carol were waiting for me at the gate.

It aint enough to get the breaks—
you gotta know how to use 'em.
Huey P. Long

They whisked me off to a Minneapolis hospital. I really didn't know what was going on, nor how close I had come to disaster. I faintly remembered being hand-cuffed the night before, and Carol and I got bills from some emergency room in Salt Lake City months later. I spent six days in the Minneapolis hospital and, once again (just like in 1989), the phone became my best friend. I don't really know what I told who, but I made dozens of calls, probably to tell family and friends about my "adventures" and how Carol had come to the rescue.

When I got out of the hospital, the computer was to glitch once more. The afternoon after getting out (I was with Carol less than 24 hours) I told her I needed to be living on my own for a while. Carol was very upset, so I just left…first thinking I would get a place across town, but when I got in the car, my mood shifted toward Milwaukee again. And off I went.

In Milwaukee, I found two jobs and an apartment in an attempt to "start my life over again." I got some provisions from a couple of friends in the area and set up house in a nearly-empty apartment.

On the second night of my second-shift job, I received a letter from Carol. She took a wild guess, based on previous employment at a franchise store and wrote in desperation. Upon reading it I became quite agitated. The shift seemed to drag on and on…and I drank cup after cup of high octane coffee. By the end of the shift my head felt like it was full of pudding. I got off a little early and headed for my apartment, and *safety*.

I had a meal and went to sleep, but only for an hour.

Waking, I got up and felt pulled to reread Carol's letter, then started to read (*for the first time)* the beginning of the *"life-changing"* 24 pages written three weeks earlier. To my dismay, the words seemed too petty, almost like a child complaining about a broken favorite toy…I looked around my nearly-empty apartment and, suddenly, the veil of delusion faded away—like a ship coming out of a fog bank! As if a curtain had lifted, I became <u>ME</u> again! I had been reconnected with my authentic inner self!

> *Your vision will become clear only*
> *when you can look into your own heart.*
> *Carl Jung*

The miracle of the fading delusion was as sudden as how I fell into depression in 1980—with just exactly the opposite result. Upon this awakening, I realized I was sick and sought help immediately. I tried to call home, but Carol had changed the number. So I packed some things and headed off for the hospital in northern Milwaukee and admitted myself.

The next morning, I made the most significant phone call of my life—I called Carol at work to tell her that I was in the hospital and realized I had been misled by the illness. She was warm and understanding, and got the ball rolling for me to come back to Minnesota. Two days later she was on a plane to Milwaukee to escort me back home.

Carol was so loving and empathetic because she knew when I was manic that "this was not me"— that the illness had changed my personality and I was no longer in control. When I called, she was so relieved to be talking to "Rich" again!

My CAIS (connectedness) had awoken me from the delusion and I had reached the calm waters once again. I immediately got a new psychiatrist who put me back on my previous regimen of medications. I now realized that to "play" with my medications, even under the guidance of a doctor, is a very serious matter. In a few days, my old meds had me back on course—yet it had only taken me about two weeks on the improper medication to become ill, causing the dangerous episode.

He who knows others is wise;
He who knows himself is
enlightened.
                    unknown

My life, our lives, were back on track, balancing
on the high wire with renewed confidence and
vigor. We had made it through the rapids and
found clear sailing on the other side. We have
learned so much from this episode—I learned
that I am a very vulnerable being and the tiger is
always in the bush. Carol learned that she could
love and support me even when I dashed our relationship on the rocks in my manic state. And, we
still have tons to learn from all of this—the learning never stops.

and the song says
　　we are prisoners
　of the prisoners we have taken
　　　　　so
　　　　often this is true
　　　　the things I believe I have
　　　total control over
　　may have control over me

such as fear
　　　I go for a long time with
　NO FEAR
　　　then suddenly I find myself
　　　　10 years back
　　　　　in seemingly the same position
　　　　　　as a far past person
　　　how can this happen?
　　　　haven't I outgrown this?
　　　　　and security is temporarily shaken
　　　but on I go and I realize
it was just a glitch ~

and even with this I can learn
　　　　　　　(isn't that the point?)
　　　　　so I choose to learn
　　　　and plan
　　　and let go of the controls
　　　(to the will of God)

　　　　　　　jacob

Chapter Six: Balance

Will I run or will I fly
take root, seek shelter or water to swim
see sun set or rise or disappear into lofty cloud?

It takes a keen eye and open ear
to know when the journey calls for change
do I choose safety in numbers
or risk being the lone rider on desert trails?

Only God knows which way is best to turn
to sprout...to reach...to duck...or run
God sees the way within me
if only I quiet myself enough to hear
the soothing voice of silence inside

"Fix it, God! Just fix it!"— *yells my anxious self*
where troubles sit and churn & burn
But I hear God say, "No need to worry—
trust, listen and wait for Me…"
so I set my ego, will and anxiety aside
and lay to rest my suffered self
I let go and fall into the open hands of God
and all will be well

jacob

Balance has many different meanings, but in all cases, being off or out of balance is not a good thing. It is a continuous journey of trial and error to maintain a healthy balance, be it emotional, physical, spiritual, social or vocational.

During the time I lived in Bozeman, Montana from 1980 to 1985, it was difficult finding long-term employment opportunities, so I hopped from job to job just to keep a roof over my head and food on the table. Because of the strong friendships I had cultivated and a great church community with which I was involved, I found a healthy social and spiritual balance, which enabled me to stay emotionally balanced. Physically, I thrived. My mode of transportation was a bicycle so I got adequate exercise and eating right kept me physically strong.

In the fall of 1985, a special friend of mine found a job for himself out in the San Francisco area. We had become quite close and the thought of seeing him leave was unbearable. He suggested I move out to California, where I could finish my hair cutting course, which I had begun in Bozeman.

So off I went to California, not knowing the drastic difference of pace in lifestyle to which I would need to adapt. I must mention that I was not taking my medications on a regular basis and did not know that all the new changes in my life could set me up for disaster.

I started haircutting school in September, got a part time job at a bank in San Francisco, commuting by bus and BART (Bay Area Rapid Transit) between home, school, work and home. The slow pace of Montana life had now flip-flopped to the hectic non-stop pace of California. Within six weeks I crashed into a brick wall of depression and psychotic episodes that landed me back in a county hospital in my home state, Minnesota, with only a suitcase of clothes to my name.

> *To be alive is power existing*
> *in itself, without a further function,*
> *omnipotence enough.*
> **Emily Dickenson**

Once again, my life was out of balance and the only way to regain my mental stability was through a stay at the hospital (which lasted 5 weeks) and getting me back on track with my medications, which I had forgotten was one of the crucial components of my life balance.

Well, it was back to life's drawing board, to rebuild and reestablish myself in Minnesota. I was released from the hospital and lived, for several months, at half-way a house for people who were mentally & physically challenged—who were in transition. I worked for a temp agency and gradually felt confident enough to look for full time employment.

Through the department of jobs and rehabilitation, I located a full time job, and found a home to share with a young lady I met at church.

I was blessed to find a "career" in 1987 as an employee benefits broker and, to this date, have a fulfilling vocation in this industry. As mentioned in chapter two, many opportunities have arisen, through conversations with clients, to share my knowledge and experience as a mental health consumer. This has proven to be a valuable and reassuring resource to customers and their loved ones who have or live with those with a mental illness.

> *We must be true to ourselves*
> *before we can know a truth*
> *outside us.*
> *Thomas Merton*

Although being mentally and emotionally in balance is vital to my health, any other major area, when disrupted, can also have a serious negative affect on my life balance as well.

About five years ago, I had a major disaster being caught literally "physically" off balance. During a dress rehearsal at church for an Easter program, I had to cross behind the choir risers, in the dark, on a stage about four feet off the gym floor, to get to a microphone for my solo spot. As I blindly scurried around the risers, I tripped over a speaker and ended up falling off the back end of the stage, with my foot wrapped around a two-by-four up on the stage.

The show must go on, but I didn't, as I ended up in surgery to "pin" my ankle back together. I spent the next six weeks in a cast, the first three weeks of which were spent recuperating in my home town, at Mom and Dad's. Once again, I was their little girl, needing assistance with virtually all every day tasks, from washing my hair to cooking my meals, to helping me to the bathroom.

*May you have just enough clouds
in your life to make a beautiful
sunset.*

> *unknown*

My ankle eventually healed, but not without tipping my life out of balance, temporarily. The beautiful part of this whole experience was how my life slowed down, allowing me to take another breath of the gentle love and care of Mom and Dad, not unlike that which I experienced as a child, growing up. Not many years later, my mother passed away and the time spent with them, with my ankle in the air, was worth every ache and pain. The memories of those weeks of quality time with my parents still warm my heart and fill it with gratitude.

Regardless of what the imbalance, be it physical or mental, it takes time and constant care to regain, maintain and sustain that delicate balance.

Rich created a balancing tool he calls the *Connectedness Tree,* which brings together what he considers the 12 basic components of human life. The roots are grounded in the *meaning of life* (philosophy) and spirituality, bridged to the other areas by *attitude*—how one treats life.

If any area is neglected, one's life can be thrown off-kilter, and dysfunction may arise. (Neither Rich nor I are psychologists, so we can only speak for ourselves as mental health consumers, and persons with bipolar disorder.) If a person concentrates too much on career and financial gain, the socio-emotional and recreational/avocational areas may be deprived. Whereas, if a person concentrates only on the psychological and emotional, the physical (diet and exercise) may suffer.

Such an imbalance can be particularly dangerous for a person with bipolar—even more so than a person without it. It's kind of like a delicate rose bush needing to be covered to avoid the frost...people with bipolar are susceptible to falling out of the boat more easily if balance is shaken.

Chapter six's acronym is:

FLIP
    Fully
      Living
        In the
          Present

One of the ways I have fought to live in the present through the years is by waging a fight against the "battle of the bulge". Lose weight—maintain for a short time—gain the weight back—plus a few additional pounds....It has been said, by professionals who prescribe medications used to treat depression and bipolar illness, that taking such medications can cause weight gain. Both Rich and I are living proof of that statement. In December of 1999, I made the decision to lose the extra 65 pounds I had been carrying around much too long. In the first two and a half months, I lost 20 pounds by following one of the popular "protein

diets," but soon found out that virtually cutting out a whole food group (carbohydrates) was not healthy for me. Carbohydrates are referred to as "brain food" and I soon found out that the lack of them in my diet had caused a considerable decline in my capacity to cope with stress created by the multi-task, detail-oriented job I have.

I happened to tune into the local public television program one night when Dr. Andrew Weil was teaching on nutrition and just plain eating a healthy diet. I quickly went out and purchased his book on CD and listened to the wealth of knowledge he had to offer. My love for cooking took a new turn for the better and soon I was making tasty, healthy, nutritious, *balanced,* meals. The local natural foods store provides me with many wonderful ingredients and ideas for eating healthily.

By June of 2000, six months after starting my weight loss quest, the scale read 45 pounds lighter! I am about two thirds of the way to my goal weight (suggested by my doctor). The challenge to maintain a healthy weight will always be before me, but I now feel in control and better able to listen to what my body needs versus what it wants.

Weight control is just one part (physical) of the *Connectedness Tree* into which I have put my effort. It has made me more conscious of the decisions I make everyday that affect my balance. The components of *The Tree* are all interconnected and one choice toward health in one area can be beneficial to other parts.

> *The change of one simple*
> *behavior can affect other*
> *behaviors and thus change*
> *many things.*
> *Jean Baer*

Connectedness Tree

social-relational family

vocational/job/career physical

psychological intellectual/educational

recreational & avocational "maintenance"

financial & economic emotional

a
t
t
i
t
u
d
e

connectedness

values, beliefs

principles, meaning

symbolism

spirituality

By attempting to live fully in the moment, with gratitude and optimism, I'm convinced my choices will move me toward health.

I remember
        the joy of solid solitude
        to be alive and in the air and water
        swimming in a body free from chains
or molasses stick
in the mud

and bird without feather
oh yes I remember
        that feeling of being free

                jacob

Chapter Seven: The Social Life

I am who I am
what I am
where I am
because of my struggles
suffering
but I don't go back and greet
those who shut me out
and labeled me unacceptable

I don't go back and chum with
the ones who smashed
my free-flowing
friendship on the
rocks of jealousy
I can only forgive them and
thank God for giving me
the wisdom and TOLERANCE
to keep travlin' on

jacob

Who holds the ends of the tight ropes people with manic-depression walk? Our support persons. We are, in part, formed by our relationships...friends, family, co-workers, supervisors, even acquaintances. Chapter seven's acronym is NICE:

Navigating
Interpersonal
Communications
Effectively

We choose our friends, in a way that we never chose our families.

In the end, good friendships
are the true sustaining force.
Joan Frank

I remember making my first best friend;. it happened in 9th grade, and, ironically, came about with a classmate I knew since grade school. Christopher and I often fought, verbally, years before, and had had NO time for one another. But in ninth grade we began to see that we were pretty similar and started *hangin' out.* Having a *best friend* made a big difference in my self-worth because, finally, I had another guy my age to relate to—to spend time with, without having to search the world over for a companion.

Good friends can come in the form of brothers too. I, a few years ago, mailed about 25 supplemental form letters describing a spiritual experience I had just had. They were in the form of a stream of consciousness journal entry. When my brother got it he called to see if I was all right, because he thought the letter was quite inappropriate and even strange—possibly *manic*. When I got the call, I was expecting affirmation and got the opposite—I immediately realized that it was kind of a manic letter and that it had been sent on a whim. It took guts and love for my brother to call. This was a turning point in the life of my illness. Never again have I sent a "mass mailing" without thoroughly thinking it over.

> *A candle loses nothing by*
> *lighting another candle.*
> *Fr. James Keller*

One of the struggles I have had in past years was building a life I was proud of—so that I could share it with others. You see, my belief is that much of who we are as humans is built on our preferences—what we like and dislike, agree with or disagree with. And the ability to share them is what makes up much of our social interaction. Just listen in on a conversation and pick out the preferences and commonalities being shared—they are usually ever-present. "I like THIS job, I don't like THAT TV show—I really like THIS sweater, I really hate THAT feeling...!"

If this is true, then we are, in a sense, our opinions—our feelings and decisions. Therefore, to be an interesting person, we need to have hobbies, pastimes, preferences that give us something to talk about. THIS is what was missing many times in my life.

> *If we know ourselves, we're always*
> *home—anywhere.*
> *Glinda, The Wiz*

Since 1982, I have spent ample time *getting to know myself* through journaling. On paper, I have found what interests me and have gone out to find fulfillment through action. Carol and I both showed interest in canoeing and, two years ago, bought one to glide over nearby (and not-so-nearby) lakes. This has given us many enjoyable times to share. It's an example of our interpersonal communications being enhanced by a preference, as we share with others our adventures in the canoe on a northern lake in the summer.

As mentioned in the poem at the beginning of this chapter, I don't spend time blaming and shaming those who have been cruel or unfair to me. But I also don't go back and waste precious time trying to change their minds. A good friend of mine once told me that he is very particular about those with whom he INVESTS his time and that he will not waste it on negative or fruitless relationships.

The best way to destroy your enemy
is to make him your friend.
Abe Lincoln

You may be wondering what this has to do with bipolar disorder—Everything! Emotional and social stability, buttressed by our interpersonal relationships, can (and do) create an important part of balance for all of us. And, as we mentioned earlier, the balance for people with bipolar depends even more on relationships.

For myself, my mom was THE crucial link to sanity that helped pull me through my first bout with depression my senior year in high school, in

1980. Twenty one years later, she is still a major stabilizing force in my recovery. In 1980, I remember her taking ample time to listen to me, or just be with me when I couldn't express my horrors. She taught me the importance of the power of *presence—being there* for others...not necessarily having all the brilliant answers or swift sound bites of wisdom, but just listening and showing love through her *presence.*

Treat people as assets to be
developed rather than costs to cut.
Robert Riech

My feeling is that our relationships are the most important assets we will ever have...but I didn't always believe this. In 1985, a friend of mine traveled to California to visit her boyfriend at the same time I had purchased a new bike—each costing about $350. My attitude at the time was that my investment was more lasting (and sensible)...after all, when her trip was over, my bike would still be in my hands, and her trip would be but a memory. It took my sliding on oil and falling in the middle of a busy intersection in Milwaukee to see that my bike could go away at any time—and so could my health! And my friends time and money spent on her California trip would—relationship-wise—last forever. I had to eat crow on that occasion, but it sure taught me a great lesson..."love people and use things," as speaker Will Rogers once put it.

> *Our greatest glory consists not in*
> *never falling, but in rising every*
> *time we fall.*
> *Ralph Waldo Emerson*

My relationship with Carol is my greatest stabilizing force, and the most rewarding encounter I have ever had. Since we met, with the open knowledge of our mutual illness, we have had a foundation of basic understanding since the start. We take relationships seriously, as if priceless gems set in our outstretched hands—creating joy and bringing responsibility to nurture them tenderly. We thank God often for the wonderful people we have in our lives who promote our health through loving, positive interaction.

pathways
from here to there
and i am thankful
for the guidance of a loving God
who sends me
and encourages me
and provides the light at the end of the tunnel
so I may continue to grow beyond my present limits
oh how wonderful it is to be on the path
way on down the long road
in search of my self
seeking the authentic life
some call it soul searching
(i think it is much more)
to be aware of the self
watching, listening, feeling, touching
is to know the soul
and how important it is to observe and breathe in
the words, actions, feelings of others
and encourage them to be their best selves
what a blessed mission
this i call
creatively building souls
the results of such depth of love are many and
wondrous
for who can tell who we will influence positively
like nature's helicopters spinning down
from a generous autumn branch

to hungry earth below
as small seed may produce a majestic tree
(such is with each of our relationships)
many are the mysteries of life we meet
upon our
pathways

jacob

Epilogue

In this book, Carol and I have shared some of the most vulnerable details about our lives with bipolar. Why? Because we believe it is through communicating these details that we not only inform others about the illness, but truly understand it ourselves. Some may say we are taking a big risk in divulging such personal information. But we believe we would be taking an even greater risk by NOT sharing... the risk of missing the opportunity to inform others about the "ups and downs" of bipolar and how to live and thrive with a mental illness. We hope that *Bipolar Balancing Act* has been encouraging and enlightening for you.

Rich and Carol

Appendix

Manic Clues

1. Urgency
2. Destructive of Relationships
3. Heightened Energy_
4. Quick to Anger
5. Tunnel Vision
6. Destructive of Things
7. Driving faster/Recklessly
8. Doing EVERYTHING faster
9. Feel Called to the Extraordinary
10. Euphoric, No Matter What Happens
11. Inappropriate/Unrealistic Elation
12. Lose Importance of/Avoid Medications
13. "Racing Thoughts"
14. Disturbed Ability to Make Decisions
15. Everything is "FUN!"
16. Flow of Creative Ideas is Continuous
17. Delusive
18. Destructive of Self/Belongings

19. Sense of New-Found Power
20. Manipulative/Aggressive
21. One Does Not Recognize Any of the Above as Abnormal or that it Even Exists

Depressive Clues

1. Low mood, down in the dumps
2. Avoidance (of everything)
3. Unable to focus attention
4. Hopelessness
5. Preoccupied with negative thoughts
6. Indecisive
7. Sleep more/eat more
8. Avoid physical activity
9. Destructive daydreaming
10. Don't want to put out ANY effort

Author Biography

Rich and Carol met because they shared a common ailment, manic-depression, and were both willing to talk about it.

0-595-22755-4